A CENTURY *of*
NEWPORT

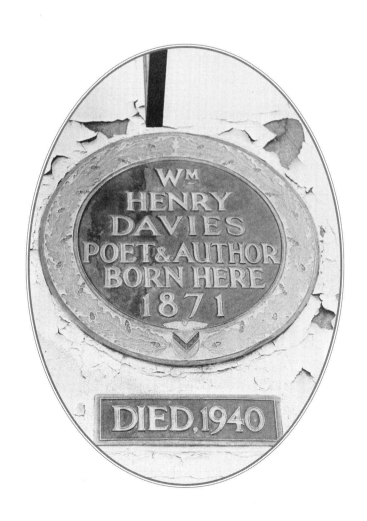

The High Street in 1958 – unpedestrianised, but still almost traffic-free. (*Western Mail and Echo*)

A CENTURY *of* NEWPORT

JOHN O'SULLIVAN

SUTTON PUBLISHING

First published in the United Kingdom in 2000 by
Sutton Publishing Limited · Phoenix Mill
Thrupp · Stroud · Gloucestershire · GL5 2BU

British Library Cataloguing in Publication Data
A catalogue record for this book is available from the British Library.

ISBN 0-7509-2651-1

Front endpaper: Aerial view of the River Usk, 1970s. (*Terry Soames*)
Back endpaper: Aerial view of Newport, 1947. (*Western Mail and Echo*)
Half title page: Plaque in memory of Newport's poet tramp, W.H. Davies. (*Western Mail and Echo*)
Title page: The Westgate Hotel, scene of the Chartist rioting of 1839. (*Western Mail and Echo*)

 Published in association with **WHSmith**

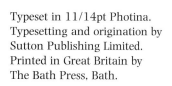

*This book is dedicated to my sons,
Dominic and the late John Joseph,
both born in Newport*

Typeset in 11/14pt Photina.
Typesetting and origination by
Sutton Publishing Limited.
Printed in Great Britain by
The Bath Press, Bath.

The Green Man statue in tribute to super tramp W.H. Davies. (*Western Mail and Echo*)

Contents

Newport High Street in 1966, the year the first Severn Bridge opened. (*Western Mail and Echo*)

Britain: A Century of Change

Two women encumbered with gas masks go about their daily tasks during the early days of the war. (*Hulton Getty Picture Collection*)

The sixty years ending in 1900 were a period of huge trans-
formation for Britain. Railway stations, post-and-telegraph offices,
police and fire stations, gasworks and gasometers, new livestock
markets and covered markets, schools, churches, football grounds,
hospitals and asylums, water pumping stations and sewerage plants
totally altered the urban scene, and the country's population tripled with
more than seven out of ten people being born in or moving to the
towns. The century that followed, leading up to the Millennium's end in
2000, was to be a period of even greater change.

When Queen Victoria died in 1901, she was measured for her coffin
by her grandson Kaiser Wilhelm, the London prostitutes put on black
mourning and the blinds came down in the villas and terraces spreading
out from the old town centres. These centres were reachable by train
and tram, by the new bicycles and still newer motor cars, were con-
nected by the new telephone, and lit by gas or even electricity. The shops
may have been full of British-made cotton and woollen clothing but the
grocers and butchers were selling cheap Danish bacon, Argentinian
beef, Australasian mutton and tinned or dried fish and fruit from
Canada, California and South Africa. Most of these goods were carried
in British-built-and-crewed ships burning Welsh steam coal.

As the first decade moved on, the Open Spaces Act meant more parks,
bowling greens and cricket pitches. The First World War transformed
the place of women, as they took over many men's jobs. Its other
legacies were the war memorials which joined the statues of Victorian
worthies in main squares round the land. After 1918 death duties and
higher taxation bit hard, and a quarter of England changed hands in
the space of only a few years.

The multiple shop – the chain store – appeared in the high street:
Sainsburys, Maypole, Lipton's, Home & Colonial, the Fifty Shilling Tailor,
Burton, Boots, W.H. Smith. The shopper was spoilt for choice, attracted
by the brash fascias and advertising hoardings for national brands like
Bovril, Pears Soap, and Ovaltine. Many new buildings began to be seen,
such as garages, motor showrooms, picture palaces (cinemas), 'palais de
dance', and ribbons of 'semis' stretched along the roads and new
bypasses and onto the new estates nudging the green belts.

During the 1920s cars became more reliable and sophisticated as well
as commonplace, with developments like the electric self-starter making
them easier for women to drive. Who wanted to turn a crank handle in
the new short skirt? This was, indeed, the electric age as much as the
motor era. Trolley buses, electric trams and trains extended mass
transport and electric light replaced gas in the street and the home,
which itself was groomed by the vacuum cleaner.

A major jolt to the march onward and upward was administered by
the Great Depression of the early 1930s. The older British industries –

textiles, shipbuilding, iron, steel, coal – were already under pressure from foreign competition when this worldwide slump arrived. Luckily there were new diversions to alleviate the misery. The 'talkies' arrived in the cinemas; more and more radios and gramophones were to be found in people's homes; there were new women's magazines, with fashion, cookery tips and problem pages; football pools; the flying feats of women pilots like Amy Johnson; the Loch Ness Monster; cheap chocolate and the drama of Edward VIII's abdication.

Things were looking up again by 1936 and new light industry was booming in the Home Counties as factories struggled to keep up with the demand for radios, radiograms, cars and electronic goods, including the first television sets. The threat from Hitler's Germany meant rearmament, particularly of the airforce, which stimulated aircraft and aero engine firms. If you were lucky and lived in the south, there was good money to be earned. A semi-detached house cost £450, a Morris Cowley £150. People may have smoked like chimneys but life expectancy, since 1918, was up by 15 years while the birth rate had almost halved.

In some ways it is the little memories that seem to linger longest from the Second World War: the kerbs painted white to show up in the

A W.H.Smith shop front in Beaconsfield, 1922.

blackout, the rattle of ack-ack shrapnel on roof tiles, sparrows killed by bomb blast. The biggest damage, apart from London, was in the south-west (Plymouth, Bristol) and the Midlands (Coventry, Birmingham). Postwar reconstruction was rooted in the Beveridge Report which set out the expectations for the Welfare State. This, together with the nationalisation of the Bank of England, coal, gas, electricity and the railways, formed the programme of the Labour government in 1945.

Children collecting aluminium to help the war effort, London, 1940s. (*IWM*)

Times were hard in the late 1940s, with rationing even more stringent than during the war. Yet this was, as has been said, 'an innocent and well-behaved era'. The first let-up came in 1951 with the Festival of Britain and there was another fillip in 1953 from the Coronation, which incidentally gave a huge boost to the spread of TV. By 1954 leisure motoring had been resumed but the Comet – Britain's best hope for taking on the American aviation industry – suffered a series of mysterious crashes. The Suez debacle of 1956 was followed by an acceleration in the withdrawal from Empire, which had begun in 1947 with the Independence of India. Consumerism was truly born with the advent of commercial TV and most homes soon boasted washing machines, fridges, electric irons and fires.

A street party to celebrate the Queen's Coronation, June 1953. (*Hulton Getty Picture Collection*)

The *Lady Chatterley* obscenity trial in 1960 was something of a straw in the wind for what was to follow in that decade. A collective loss of inhibition seemed to sweep the land, as the Beatles and the Rolling Stones transformed popular music, and retailing, cinema and the theatre were revolutionised. Designers, hairdressers, photographers and models moved into places vacated by an Establishment put to flight by the new breed of satirists spawned by *Beyond the Fringe* and *Private Eye*.

In the 1970s Britain seems to have suffered a prolonged hangover after the excesses of the previous decade. Ulster, inflation and union troubles were not made up for by entry into the EEC, North Sea Oil, Women's Lib or, indeed, Punk Rock. Mrs Thatcher applied the corrective in the 1980s,

as the country moved more and more from its old manufacturing base over to providing services, consulting, advertising, and expertise in the 'invisible' market of high finance or in IT.

The post-1945 townscape has seen changes to match those in the worlds of work, entertainment and politics. In 1952 the Clean Air Act served notice on smogs and pea-souper fogs, smuts and blackened buildings, forcing people to stop burning coal and go over to smokeless sources of heat and energy. In the same decade some of the best urban building took place in the 'new towns' like Basildon, Crawley, Stevenage and Harlow. Elsewhere open warfare was declared on slums and what was labelled inadequate, cramped, back-to-back, two-up, two-down, housing. The new 'machine for living in' was a flat in a high-rise block. The architects and planners who promoted these were in league with the traffic engineers, determined to keep the motor car moving whatever the price in multi-storey car parks, meters, traffic wardens and ring roads. The old pollutant, coal smoke, was replaced by petrol and diesel exhaust, and traffic noise.

Fast food was no longer only a pork pie in a pub or fish-and-chips. There were Indian curry houses, Chinese take-aways and American-style ham- burgers, while the drinker could get away from beer in a wine bar. Under the impact of television

Punk rockers demonstrate their anarchic style during the 1970s. (*Barnaby's Picture Library*)

the big Gaumonts and Odeons closed or were rebuilt as multi-screen cinemas, while the palais de dance gave way to discos and clubs.

From the late 1960s the introduction of listed buildings and conserv- ation areas, together with the growth of preservation societies, put a brake on 'comprehensive redevelopment'. The end of the century and the start of the Third Millennium see new challenges to the health of towns and the wellbeing of the nine out of ten people who now live urban lives. The fight is on to prevent town centres from dying, as patterns of housing and shopping change, and edge-of-town super- markets exercise the attractions of one-stop shopping. But as banks and department stores close, following the haberdashers, greengrocers, butchers and ironmongers, there are signs of new growth such as farmers' markets, and corner stores acting as pick-up points where customers collect shopping ordered on-line from web sites.

Futurologists tell us that we are in stage two of the consumer revolu- tion: a shift from mass consumption to mass customisation driven by a

Millennium celebrations over the Thames at Westminster, New Year's Eve, 1999. (*Barnaby's Picture Library*)

desire to have things that fit us and our particular lifestyle exactly, and for better service. This must offer hope for small city-centre shop premises, as must the continued attraction of physical shopping, browsing and being part of a crowd: in a word, 'shoppertainment'. Another hopeful trend for towns is the growth in the number of young people postponing marriage and looking to live independently, alone, where there is a buzz, in 'swinging single cities'. Theirs is a 'flats-and-cafés' lifestyle, in contrast to the 'family suburbs', and certainly fits in with government's aim of building 60 per cent of the huge amount of new housing needed on 'brown' sites, recycled urban land. There looks to be plenty of life in the British town yet.

Newport: An Introduction

Newport is a cradle of democracy, among its more prosaic claims to fame as a busy seaport and industrial town. It was a centre for radical thinking at the dawn of the Industrial Revolution, and the Chartist riots of 1839 helped spark the revolution which eventually led to votes for all, although women had to wait for decades after the right was granted to men. The Newport Chartists paid a high price with twenty killed by troops in a battle outside the Westgate Hotel, where bullet scars can still be seen.

The leader of the Newport rising of 4 November 1839 was John Frost, who was born in Newport in 1784 and died in 1877. Frost was a draper in Newport, was elected to the first town council in 1835 and held the office of Mayor in 1836/37. He became involved in the Chartist movement, a political reform group of working-class origin, and took part in the 1839 uprising.

An artist's impression of the Chartists rioting on 4 November 1839. (*Western Mail and Echo*)

In 1840 Frost was convicted of high treason and sentenced to death. Instead of being hanged he was exiled for life to Van Diemen's Land, now Tasmania. He was allowed to return to Britain in 1854, and his name is remembered in John Frost Square, Newport, the scene of many events and celebrations throughout the twentieth century. It is there that you will find the Newport Museum and Art Gallery, a treasure house of relics which tell the story of the town.

It is a story which is linked to Caerleon, one of the richest archaeological sites in Britain. Caerleon, on the bank of the River Usk, was the Roman fortress of Isca, which together with York and Chester was one of the permanent Roman Legionary fortresses in Britain. The Caerleon fortress was founded around AD 75 and remained a military base until the end of the third century. Archaeological digs enable visitors to see how the Romans lived nearly two millennia ago. Legend has it that Caerleon is the site of King Arthur's Round Table, though it is by no means alone in that claim.

Although Newport's commercial history can be traced back to the twelfth century, it grew into one of the most important ports along the Bristol Channel in the nineteenth century, with the development of the coalfields in the neighbouring valleys. While Cardiff's investment was provided by the Butes, Newport's mentor was Viscount Tredegar, whose money helped create one of the most up-to-date docks in Britain. The Alexandra Docks included a deep-sea lock which was 1,000ft long and 100ft wide, one of the largest in the world. The docks became important for exporting coal, an activity which ended in 1964 when the trade was transferred to Barry. Later in the century Newport became one of the main ports for exporting cars. The other major link was to the Spencer Works at Llanwern, one of the biggest steelworks in the world. As this book was going to press a shadow of uncertainty hung over the works, which had been a cornerstone of the Newport economy for decades.

A landmark of which Newport is justly proud is the Transporter Bridge, which has carried cars over the River Usk for decades. It was opened in 1906 to link the busy maritime activities on the east and west banks of the Usk. The decision to establish a transporter bridge was taken after engineers said that the exceptionally high tides and the volume of trade made a ferry or swing bridge impracticable.

Newport's religious roots can be traced back to the first millennium, when the church of St Woolos, which is the Latin form of the Welsh saint Gwynllyn, was formed. The tower of the church was built by Jasper Tudor, Earl of Pembroke and uncle of Henry VII, who died in 1495. Separating the tower from the main body of the church is the Chapel of St Mary. Between this and the nave is a Norman arch, considered to be one of the most remarkable in Britain. At the time of

Newport's famous Transporter Bridge. (*Western Mail and Echo*)

the Disestablishment of the Church in Wales from the Church in England in 1921, St Woolos was named as the Pro-Cathedral to serve the new diocese of Monmouth. In 1930 it was named as the Cathedral Church.

On 7 December 1999 the Rt Revd Rowan Williams, Bishop of Monmouth, was elected as the eleventh Archbishop of Wales, and a few weeks later he was enthroned at St Woolos Cathedral. Archbishop Rowan was born in the Swansea valley in 1950. His studies took him to Christ Church, Cambridge, Oxford and the theological training college of the Resurrection at Mirfield. He was ordained a deacon in 1977 and a priest in 1978. After a succession of teaching posts at Cambridge and Oxford he became Bishop of Monmouth in 1991, and is seen as one of the Anglican Church's most stimulating thinkers.

Since the influx of the Irish in the middle of the nineteenth century, Newport has been a major centre of Catholicism. St Mary's Church, on Stow Hill, was being built at the time of the Chartist riots in 1939. The Rosminian priests cared for and buried the cholera victims during the major outbreaks of the nineteenth century. Around the second millennium, the church is still going strong. Llantarnam Abbey, an old Cistercian monastery on the outskirts of Newport, is the Provincial

House of the sisters of St Joseph of Annécy, who have served Newport in the fields of education, nursing and social work for more than 130 years.

Until 1915 Newport was the main Roman Catholic centre in Wales, with Bishop Hedley holding the title of Bishop of Newport. His successor was given the title of Archbishop of Cardiff. When the Rt Revd Daniel Mullins was appointed Auxiliary Bishop of Cardiff in 1970 he opted to take the title of Bishop of Newport, but the Vatican told him he was too late. The title had already been given to the famous American author and broadcaster Bishop Fulton Sheen, who visited the town in the 1970s.

The importance of Newport at the beginning of the twentieth century would have come as a surprise to Fr Burke, a Catholic priest who was based at Usk in 1827. He left Usk after a year for reasons outlined in a letter to Biship Collingridge: 'although I fear that Newport can never be made as good a Mission as Usk, and though I know it to be usual, if particular reasons to the contrary cannot be assigned, to remove clergymen from a worse to a better situation, yet in the event of a change, I should for many reasons prefer Newport. I am a young man and know the necessity of employment. In Newport I have a good congregation, and Pontypool, I dare say, will go with it. Nearly all the Catholics in Newport are Irish and in Pontypool also. I speak the Irish language.'

Throughout the nineteenth and twentieth centuries Irish people played a prominent part in the development of Newport, although they were accepted with reluctance when they came as refugees from the Irish famine of the 1840s. When permission was refused for them to land on shore they left a ship called the *Wanderer* at the mouth of the River Usk and crawled over the mud to reach land. In part of Newport the Irish are still known as the Mud Crawlers.

Like other parts of South Wales, Newport was pounded by the Luftwaffe during the Second World War, but it was two remarkable stories relating to the sea that earned the town a place in history. The crew of the submarine *Turbulent* was commanded by Newport-born John 'Tubby' Linton. It sank a number of German ships, including a cruiser, a destroyer, a submarine and twenty-eight supply vessels. Gunners on the *Turbulent* also destroyed three enemy trains. Commander Linton was awarded the Victoria Cross posthumously after the *Turbulent* was destroyed, with the loss of its crew of sixty, in a minefield off Corsica in 1943.

The story of the *Anglo Saxon*, which sailed from Newport with a cargo of coal for Argentina on 6 August 1940, was one of the most remarkable of any war at sea. The ship was sunk by the Germans in the Atlantic. Only two members of the crew survived – after spending

St Woolos Cathedral.
(*Western Mail and Echo*)

an incredible seventy days in a small jolly boat. Seven members of the crew were in the boat at the start of the journey, but only Bob Tapscott and Roy Widdicombe, both from Newport, survived the 2,200-mile journey and landed in the Bahamas. Sadly, Roy died when the ship on which he was returning to Britain was torpedoed by a German U-boat. Bob was living in Cardiff when he died in 1963.

A new chapter in the history of the town began in 1951, when the Civic Centre was opened. The building is a prominent landmark of which the borough can be proud. The murals in the hall depict aspects of the town's history and are unique features, the like of which are not reflected in any other civic centre in Wales or England.

When local government reorganisation took place in 1974, the new area covered 73 square miles. By this time the M4 link to London had been completed, placing Newport in a prominent place on the distribution corridor. The massive traffic jams which gave the town such a bad reputation in the 1950s and '60s were a thing of the past.

The pressure was eased by the building of the stylish George Street Bridge – the first cable cantilever bridge in Britain – the motorway and the Brynglas tunnels. The local council took full advantage of the new roads by setting up industrial and commercial estates and first class hotels and leisure centres at prime sites.

Newbridge-born Terry Matthews, one of the richest men in Britain, recognised the potential of Newport. He bought the former Lydia Beynon Nursing Home on the east end of the town and developed one of the best hotels, conference centres and golf course complexes in Europe, a building that towers over the motorway like some huge Mediterranean resort hotel.

What of the future? Michael Boon, who worked for the *Daily Express* and the *Western Mail*, wrote: 'Newport prides itself on being the gateway of Wales Electronics; semi-conductors and telecommunications products are just as much as part of Newport's manufacturing profile as sheets of steel. The town has become one of the leading investment locations in Britain. The jewel in the crown is LG Electronics of Korea, with plans to employ up to 2,000 people. It was the biggest single inward investment project in Europe. The stresses and strains within the economics of the Far East dented the initial thrust, but the electronics side of the business went ahead on schedule and employs more than 2,000.

Following a management buy-out, the former Inmos Plant is increasing its workforce up to 8,000. Telecommunications is another success story. Best known is Newbridge Networks, recently bought by Alcatel. The opportunities offered by the M4 corridor have resulted in the assembly of land for the development of business parks, such as Celtic Lakes and Cleppa Parks.

The story of twentieth-century Newport would not be complete without a tribute to William Henry Davies, the Newport-born tramp whose poetry ranks alongside the best of the era in which he lived. For many years he was a hobo in America and lost a leg when he jumped from a train. It was the book he wrote about those adventures, published as *The Autobiography of a Super Tramp*, which won him his fame and the admiration of the likes of George Bernard Shaw and Edward Thomas. Davies was born in 1871 and died in 1940, and in recent years a Green Man statue has been erected to his memory. It was Davies who wrote the memorable lines:

> What is this life if, full of care,
> We have no time to stand and stare?

There can scarcely be a more fitting introduction to a book such as this.

Edwardian Days

The memorial on the grave of Sir Briggs at Tredegar House. He was the horse the 2nd Baron and 1st Viscount of Tredegar rode at the Battle of Balaclava. (*Western Mail and Echo*)

This was the first motor car to be seen on the streets of Newport and it caused a sensation when it made its debut around the end of the nineteenth century. (*Gwent Record Office*)

A horse-drawn tram at Cross Hands Terminus, Chepstow Road, 1902. (*Western Mail and Echo*)

Crowds gathered after a steamroller and a steam-driven lorry were in collision on Newport Bridge. (*Gwent Record Office*)

The Hand Post Hotel in early Edwardian days. The pub is still there; the leisurely atmosphere, alas, is not. (*Western Mail and Echo*)

Stagecoaches died out long before this picture was taken outside the King's Hotel – but, as the crowds suggest, this one was drafted in for some special event. (*Western Mail and Echo*)

The hotel was renamed Kings but is still in business in the twenty-first century. The owner, Cardiff casino owner Gordon McIlroy, is seen outside in the 1990s. (*Western Mail and Echo*)

An insight into social life in Edwardian times. Staff and customers at the Tredegar Arms, 1906. (*Gwent Record Office*)

The opening of Pill police station. (*Western Mail and Echo*)

A tram in High Street in the early part of the twentieth century. (*Collection of Mrs Sexton, Grangetown, Cardiff*)

The chapels had a big influence in the area in Edwardian times. These are the elders at Ebenezer Chapel around 1907. (*Gwent Record Office*)

An estimate from the Great Western Railway Company for work associated with the building of the Transporter Bridge. (*Gwent Record Office*)

Tredegar House, now a popular centre for a variety of events. It had been the family home of Viscount Tredegar, and then a private school. (*Tredegar House, Newport*)

A rare insight into school life in Edwardian times can be found in an album of photographs from Stow Hill Boys School. The school is on the right. (*Gwent Record Office*)

Pupils at Stow Hill Boys Schoo, *c.* 1909. (*Gwent Record Office*)

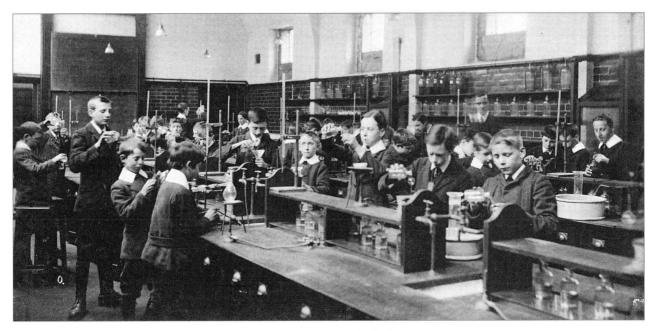

Stow Hill boys experimenting in the school laboratory. (*Gwent Record Office*)

Woodwork class at Stow Hill Boys School. (*Gwent Record Office*)

Staff at Stow Hill Boys School. (*Gwent Record Office*)

Searle & Herring's Brewery, which masked Newport Castle until the brewery was demolished. (*Gwent Record Office*)

War and Strife

By 1913 Newport was one of the top coal-exporting ports in the world. Some of the coal trucks were provided by William Buck, of Caerleon. (*Gwent Record Office*)

The drive against drink was strong in the early years of the century and Band of Hope rallies were frequently held in Newport. (*Gwent Record Office*)

Young members of the Band of Hope in Newport, *c.* 1908. (*Gwent Record Office*)

Docksmen in Newport at the time of the 1911 strike. (*Newport Library Archives*)

Reservists parading in Newport after the outbreak of war in 1914. (*Gwent Record Office*)

A military funeral at St Woolos cemetery during the First World War. (*Gwent Record Office*)

A bugler has sounded the Last Post and a volley of rifle shots are fired over the grave at St Woolos Cemetery. (*Gwent Record Office*)

Prime Minister Lloyd George addresses a meeting at Newport in 1917. (*Gwent Record Office*)

American troops disembark at Alexandra Docks in 1917. (*Newport Library Archives*)

The impressive Norman arch and chapel at St Woolos Cathedral. (*Gwent Record Office*)

Between the Wars

A Newport landmark now demolished, the clock tower on the old town hall. The man on the roof is one of the maintenance staff. (*Western Mail and Echo*)

The future King George VI, then the Duke of York, on a visit to Newport in 1924. (*Newport Library Archives*)

One of six Karrier buses which formed Newport Corporation's first fleet when it was launched in 1925. (*Western Mail and Echo*)

A show that looks well worth seeing, starring the great Welsh heart-throb. (*Western Mail and Echo*)

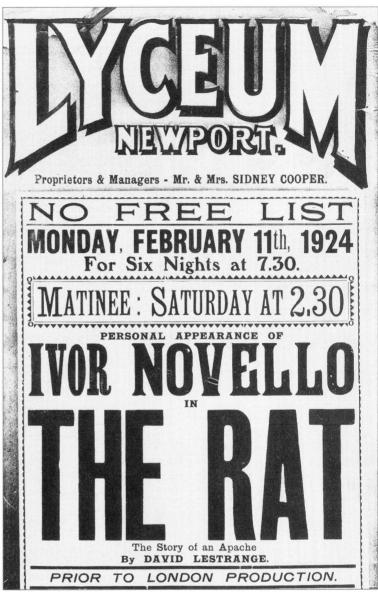

Ivor Novello was born in Cardiff.
(*Ivor Novello Foundation*)

The Minister of Transport, Colonel Ashley, officially opened Newport Bridge in 1927 in the presence of Alderman John Morgan OBE, Viscount Tredegar and the Mayor, Councillor A.T.W. James. (*Gwent Record Office*)

The High Street before the rebuilding of the post office, King's Head and other buildings, 1920. (*Mrs E. Fennell*)

The east machine shop at the Uskside Engineering Works, 1936. (*Western Mail and Echo*)

Lysaught Orb Works in the 1930s.
(*Western Mail and Echo*)

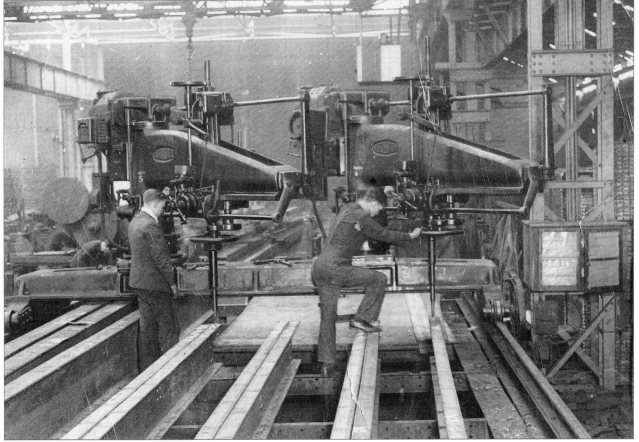

Another scene from a Newport factory in the 1930s. (*Western Mail and Echo*)

The Mayor, Alderman J.R. Wardell, opened the road over the dam of the Newport Water Scheme at Talybont on Usk. (*Western Mail and Echo*)

When John Fielding Williams VC died in 1932, he was buried in Llantarnam churchyard. He was one of eleven men who were awarded the Victoria Cross at Rorke's Drift during the Zulu War, in January 1879. (*Author*)

War Once More

Submarine Commander John 'Tubby' Linton VC, DSO. (*Western Mail and Echo*)

The crew of the submarine *Turbulent* commanded by Newport-born John 'Tubby' Linton (arrowed), who was awarded the Victoria Cross posthumously after the vessel was destroyed with the loss of its sixty crew in a minefield off Corsica in 1943. German vessels sunk by the *Turbulent* included a cruiser, a destroyer, a submarine and twenty-eight supply ships. Gunners on the *Turbulent* also destroyed three enemy trains. (*Western Mail and Echo*)

One of the most remarkable incidents during the Second World War involved two members of the crew of the *Anglo Saxon*, which left Newport with a cargo of coal for Argentina on 6 August 1940. The ship, seen above loading timber at Vancouver in 1938, was sunk by the Germans. Only two members of the crew survived – after spending seventy days in a small jolly boat. (*Ted Milburn Collection*)

The German raider *Widder*, which sank the *Anglo Saxon* in the Atlantic on 21 August 1940. (*Anthony Smith*)

Shaved and fed but still weak, seaman Robert Tapscott of Norris Street, Newport, was carried into a hospital at Nassau after spending seventy days in the jolly boat following the sinking of the *Anglo Saxon*. In the background is his fellow survivor, Roy Widdicombe of Lewis Street, Newport. Five members of the crew died during the 2,275 mile journey, the story of which is told in *Survived* by Anthony Smith, published by Quintin Smith, London (1998). (*Arthur K. Blood*)

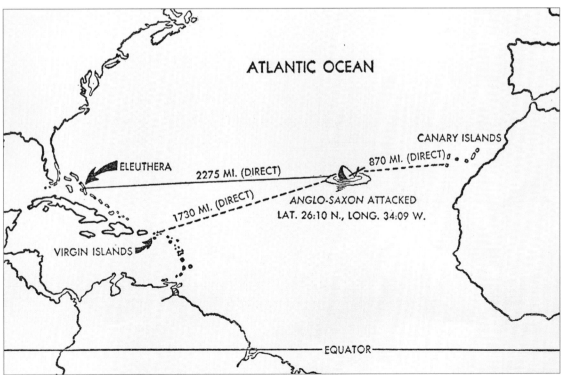

This map shows where the *Anglo Saxon* was sunk, and the 2,275-mile route the jolly boat took to Eleuthra in the Bahamas. (*Ted Milburn Collection*)

The *Anglo Saxon* jolly boat beached in the Bahamas. (*Ted Milburn Collection*)

Robert Tapscott and Roy Widdicombe posed for a photograph in the jolly boat. Roy Widdicombe sailed for Britain from New York as a passenger aboard the *Siamese Prince*, which was torpedoed off the Faro Islands in February 1941. Bob Tapscott joined the Canadian Army but settled in Cardiff after the war. He died in 1963. Newport members of the *Anglo Saxon* crew who died were: G.W. Hansen of Maesglas Grove; W. Allnatt of Maesglas Crescent; W. Prowse of Conway Road; P.J. Tackle of Hill Parade; J. Fowler of New Street; A. Eley of Victoria Avenue; F. Tenow of George Street; L. Rassmussen of Clarence Street; C. Stuart of Portland Street; G. Bedford of Hoskin Street; L.J. Morgan of William Street; T. Keyes of Hamden Road; A. Oliver of Hobin; and chief steward H. Willis. (*Ted Milburn Collection*)

Above, Barry Denny, first mate of the *Anglo Saxon*. (*Desmond C. Denny Collection*). Right, chief engineer E.E. Milburn; and below, Ted Milburn, son of the chief engineer, whose research and dedication helped bring the jolly boat back to Britain. It is now in the Imperial War Museum in London. (*Ted Milburn Collection*)

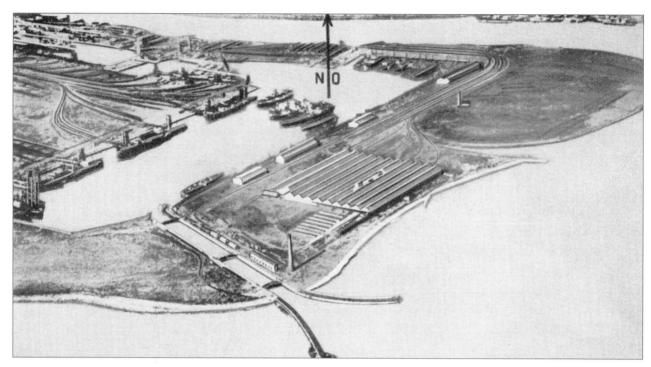

German pilots were issued with a target guide for Wales. The book featured this view of the Alexandra Docks, Newport, above, and below the steelworks on the banks of the River Usk. (*Author's collection*)

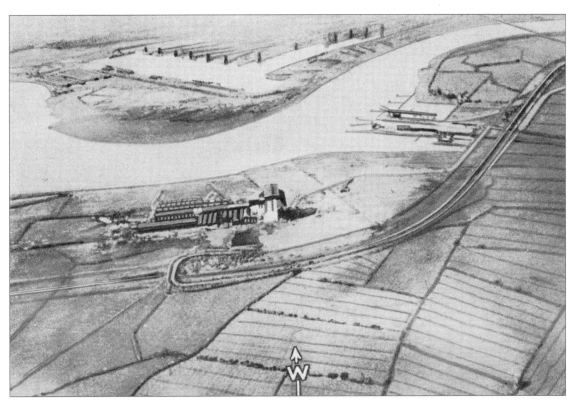

Bomb aimers were particularly interested in the riverside factories. The picture above shows the aluminium works near Alexandra Docks and the one below another view of the industrial area. (*Author's collection*)

Boy Scouts and First World War veterans were among the Air Raid Wardens in Newport in the early 1940s. (*Gwent Record Office*)

Nurses at the Royal Gwent Hospital in the 1940s. (*Western Mail and Echo*)

Corporal Edward Chapman was fighting with the
Monmouthshire Regiment on 2 April 1945 when his
group was ambushed after crossing the Dortmund–
Ems Canal. Ted Chapman was awarded the Victoria
Cross for outstanding bravery in keeping the German
troops at bay and enabling his company to capture an
important ridge – a VC who lived to tell the tale.
(*Author's collection*)

Polish troops were stationed at Newport in the 1940s. A British officer is briefing them at a local base.
(*Imperial War Museum*)

Left, dockers unload ammunition from railway trucks at Newport. It was loaded on the SS *Stanrealm*, but the destination was a secret. Below, a cache of Second World War bombs was found in Shaftesbury Street in 1971. (*Western Mail and Echo*)

Shortly before he died in 1940, a civic tribute was paid to Newport's poet tramp W.H. Davies. In his poem *Leisure* in 1911 he penned the famous words: 'What is this life, if full of care, we have no time to stand and stare?' (*Newport Library Archives*) William Henry Davies was born in 1871 and led a young life of adventure, which included many years as a hobo in America. By the time this picture was taken he had settled down and was living near Stroud in Gloucestershire with a young wife who, it was revealed after the death of both parties, he had almost literally 'picked up off the street' in London. Here, from the *Oxford Book of Quotations*, are three extracts from his works:

> Sweet Stay-at-Home, Sweet Well-content,
> Thou knowest of no strange continent
> Thou has not felt thy bosom keep
> A gentle motion with the deep
> Thou hast not sailed in Indian seas,
> Where scent comes forth in every breeze.
> *Sweet Saty-at-Home, 1913*

> It was the Rainbow gave thee birth,
> And left thee all her lovely hues.
> *Kingfisher, 1910*

> And hear the pleasant cuckoo, loud and long –
> The simple bird that thinks two notes a song.
> *April Charms, 1916*

A busy day at Newport Market between the wars. (*Western Mail and Echo*)

Civic Pride

Newport Civic Centre, which opened in the early 1950s. (*Western Mail and Echo*)

The first meeting to take place in the new council chamber, January 1951. Councillor L.F.A. Driscoll chaired the Parliamentary Improvement Committee. (*Western Mail and Echo*)

Austrian artist Hans Feibush paid a return visit to Newport in 1981 to see the murals he had painted at the Civic Centre thirty years earlier. (*Author*)

Murals in the
Civic Centre.
(*Western Mail
and Echo*)

A Festival of Britain street party in Lime Street, Pillgwenny, 1951. Two years later there would be similar
scenes for the Coronation of Queen Elizabeth II. (*Western Mail and Echo*)

When the Empire Games were held in Cardiff in 1958, the course for the marathon included Newport. This was the scene at a feeding station at Tredegar Park, a facility obviously appreciated by the veteran Ulster runner Henning. (*Western Mail and Echo*)

The start of the marathon at Cardiff Arms Park, with Tredegar Park still a long, long way away. (*Western Mail and Echo*)

Scenes from the '60s

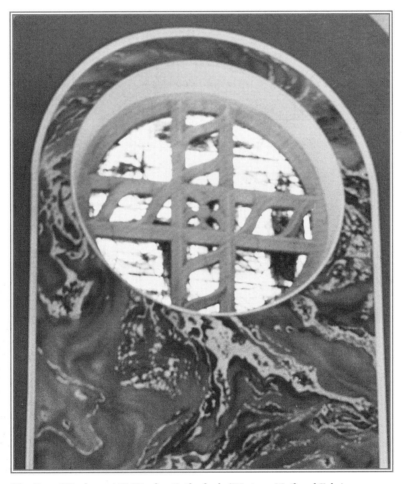

The Rose Window at St Woolos Cathedral. (*Western Mail and Echo*)

The Archbishop of Wales dedicating the Rose Window at St Woolos Cathedral, 1963. (*Western Mail and Echo*)

The Sisters of St Joseph of Annécy have been giving dedicated service to Newport for more than 130 years. Llantarnam Abbey is the Provincial House of the order, which was founded in France. There is also a convent at Stow Hill and the Sisters used to have a house at Tredegar Park. A group of nuns are seen taking their vows at Llantarnam in 1963. (*Author's collection*)

Left, Sisters of St Joseph in procession at Llantarnam in 1963, and below, in meditation. (*Author's collection*)

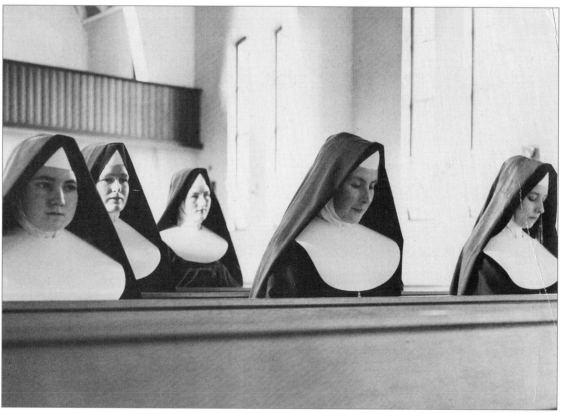

Midwives Sister Loyola and Sister Columba with babies born at St Joseph's Nursing Home, Malpas, in 1963. Below, Cardinal John Heenan, Archbishop of Westminster, gives his blessing to a new-born baby at St Joseph's. Sister Veronica is holding the baby while Sister Josephine looks on. (*Public Relations Services*)

A changing landscape with the Newport Athletic Ground. The Transporter Bridge is in the background, 1960s. (*Western Mail and Echo*)

The bridge crossing the River Usk at Caerleon. (*Western Mail and Echo*)

Jo Dominy and her daughter Betty Partridge, who campaigned about the unsafe state of the footpath on Caerleon Bridge, *c.* 1965. (*Western Mail and Echo*)

Stow Hill, with the old baths on the left and St Mary's Church on the right, 1967. (*Western Mail and Echo*)

Continental-style drinking, if not weather, came to the Lyceum Tavern in Malpas Road in 1967. (*Western Mail and Echo*)

The tug *Dunsnipe* brings the SS *Calypso* into Newport in 1965. (*Western Mail and Echo*)

Pupils of St Julian's High School and Newport High School protesting against the introduction of comprehensive education in 1966. Below, pupil Paul Richard Davies addresses the marchers before handing in a petition to Newport Borough Council. Their suggestion that 'wise men fear to tread' in comprehensive schools would seem a touch pompous to many today. (*Western Mail and Echo*)

Pupils at Rougemont private school, immune to the comprehensive system, 1966. (*Western Mail and Echo*)

J.R. Dixon, chairman of the Cleveland Bridge Company, speaking at a luncheon before the opening of the George Street Bridge in 1964. At the front of the picture is the Archbishop of Wales, the Most Revd Alfred Edwin Morris. (*Western Mail and Echo*)

The Mayor, Councillor T. Vaughan, getting ready to cut the tape at the George Street Bridge. (*Western Mail and Echo*)

The George Street Bridge, which opened in 1964. (*Western Mail and Echo*)

The Mayor's car making the inaugural journey across the George Street Bridge before the opening. Large numbers took the opportunity to walk it. (*Western Mail and Echo*)

Unloading timber from
the Russian ship *Pinega* at
Newport Docks in 1964.
(*Western Mail and Echo*)

The building of the
Brynglas Tunnels in
the mid-1960s. These
were an essential part
of the M4 at Newport.
(*Western Mail and Echo*)

The Chartist Tower dominates the Dock Street area in 1968. (*Western Mail and Echo*)

Parading before the last greyhound race at Somerton Park, October 1963. (*Western Mail and Echo*)

Selling fish at the market in 1966. At this time it had nearly 200 stalls on two levels. (*Western Mail and Echo*)

The Tredegar Hall cinema, which was later converted into the Majestic Ballroom. Welsh superstar Richard Burton tops the bill in *Bitter Victory*. (*Western Mail and Echo*)

A Newport arcade in 1967. Pedestrianised shopping malls are not such a new concept. (*Western Mail and Echo*)

The Boys' Brigade band at Pillgwenlly Carnival in the 1960s. (*Newport Library Archives*)

Times of Change

The famous Transporter Bridge in action. (*Western Mail and Echo*)

The stump of a fifteenth-century chestnut tree which can still be seen at Tredegar Park. (*Western Mail and Echo*)

The steelworks at Llanwern can be seen on the skyline in this 1973 photograph. (*Western Mail and Echo*)

Triumph sports cars lined up on the quayside at Newport in 1971, waiting to be exported to the United States. Below, a Vauxhall saloon begins its long journey. (*Leslie W. Hansen*)

When the famous American author and broadcaster Fulton Sheen was made a bishop by the Roman Catholic Church he opted for the title of Bishop of Newport. The previous holder of the title was Bishop John Cuthbert Hedley, who died in 1915, the year before the Archdiocese of Cardiff was established. Bishop Sheen visited Newport at the suggestion of the author and the Guild of Catholic Doctors. He is seen with a group of children at a Catholic primary school. (*Author's collection*)

Bishop Fulton Sheen signing the visitors' book at the Mayor's Parlour. (*Author's collection*)

Newport Market in 1975 – loon trousers and miniskirts, but still old-fashioned value. (*Western Mail and Echo*)

The former Royal Navy frigate HMS *Trowbridge* at John Cashmore's breakers' yard in Newport, August 1970. (*Western Mail and Echo*)

A scene at Newport sorting office at a time when the Post Office was adopting new technology, June 1971. (*Western Mail and Echo*)

Women street cleaners suddenly began to appear on the streets of Newport in the early 1970s. (*Western Mail and Echo*)

Edith Ford (left) and Margaret Tolley were among the first to be employed. (*Western Mail and Echo*)

Archaeologist David Zeinkowitz with a Roman cold-plunge bath, uncovered in 1978. The site contains the longest Roman swimming pool in Britain. (*Western Mail and Echo*)

Pay-as-you-enter buses were introduced in Newport in June 1971. Also in that year the town's busmen fought a successful campaign to be allowed to go to work without wearing hats. (*Western Mail and Echo*)

Newport's Phil Crump and Wolverhampton's George Hunter in a battle for points at Monmore Green in 1975. (*Western Mail and Echo*)

Into the '80s

ON NOVEMBER 4TH 1839
MORE THAN TWENTY SUPPORTERS OF THE
CHARTIST MOVEMENT, WHICH SOUGHT TO
ESTABLISH DEMOCRATIC RIGHTS FOR ALL MEN,
DIED IN AN EXCHANGE OF SHOTS AT THE
WESTGATE HOTEL NEWPORT. TEN WERE BURIED
IN THIS CHURCHYARD IN UNMARKED GRAVES.
THIS STONE IS DEDICATED TO THEIR MEMORY.

A memorial plaque to the twenty people who died in the 1839 Chartist riots. (*Western Mail and Echo*)

An artist's impression of the 1839 riots, the 150th anniversary of which was marked in 1989. (*Western Mail and Echo*)

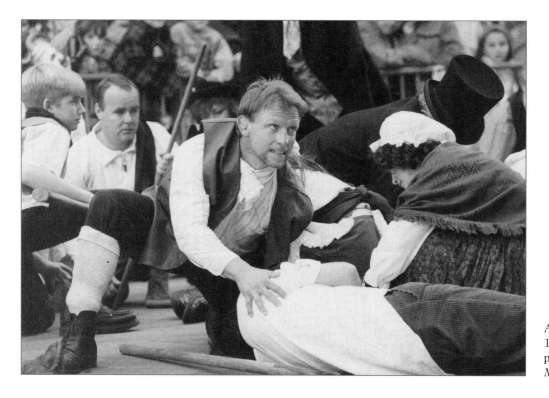

A scene from the 1989 anniversary pageant. (*Western Mail and Echo*)

Children echo the messages of the campaigners of 150 years earlier. (*Western Mail and Echo*)

Remembering the battle of 1839. (*Western Mail and Echo*)

A subway mural featuring the Chartists. (*Western Mail and Echo*)

The memorial to the Chartists outside the Westgate Hotel. (*Western Mail and Echo*)

When Archbishop John Ward of Cardiff visited St Joseph's High School in the 1980s, his pet labrador was a great favourite with the pupils. (*Author's collection*)

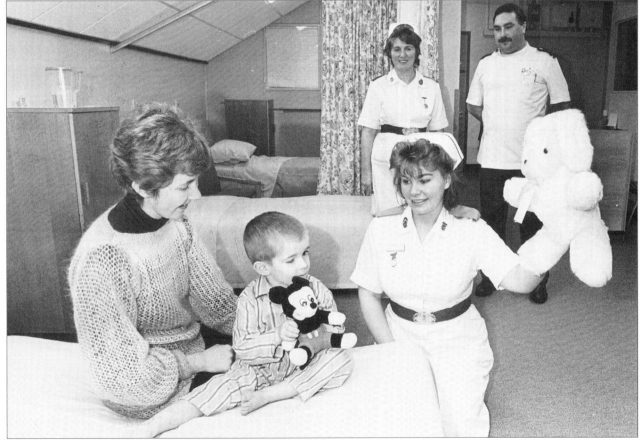

A new parent-and-baby ward opened at St Woolos Hospital in November 1988. (*Western Mail and Echo*)

The queue at the Passport Office in Newport in May 1989. (*Western Mail and Echo*)

Staff from the Newport Passport Office went on strike in June 1989 to protest about manning levels. (*Western Mail and Echo*)

Civil servants catching up on the backlog of applications following a dispute at Newport Passport Office. Far greater problems arose in the late 1990s, when the installation of new computers caused chaos. (*Western Mail and Echo*)

In 1989 the Secretary of State Peter Walker laid the foundation stone for the £16.5 million Patent Office at Newport. (*Western Mail and Echo*)

The then Labour leader Neil Kinnock and his wife Glenys with the Mayor, Councillor Trevor Warren, and Mayoress Kay Warren at the opening of the leisure centre in 1985. (*Western Mail and Echo*)

Sports Council for Wales chairman John Powell, left, handed a cheque for £30,000 to the Mayor, Councillor Trevor Warren, at the nearly completed leisure centre in October 1990. (*Western Mail and Echo*)

Totally tropical taste – almost. The pool at Newport Leisure Centre, 1985. (*Western Mail and Echo*)

A dolphin performing at Maindy Pool, Newport, late 1980s. Such performances are frowned upon these days. (*Newport Library Archives*)

More than £70,000 worth of cannabis was seized by custom officers from the *Jamaica Producer*, which docked at Newport in April 1980. A tip-off led to the discovery of the 80 lb of drugs, which was brought to Wales without the knowledge of the ship's owners. (*Western Mail and Echo*)

A 1987 view of a bank of the River Usk, pictured from the George Street Bridge. (*Western Mail and Echo*)

The remains of an ancient boat found by Glamorgan and Gwent Archaeological Trust at Barlands Farm on the River Usk, 1987. (*Western Mail and Echo*)

Another ancient boat, the *Tredunnock*, was found by the Glamorgan and Gwent Archaeological Trust at Newbridge-on-Usk, 1989. (*Western Mail and Echo*)

There was no shortage of bidders when Newport County AFC had to auction its belongings in 1989. The ground had been reclaimed by the council because the club could not afford to pay the rent. There seem to be thin pickings in the groundsmen's equipment for those intent on a souvenir of the old Ambers. (*Western Mail and Echo*)

The Mayor, Councillor Trevor Warren, being interviewed by presenter Jon Deacons for the Royal Gwent Hospital Radio in September 1985. (*Richard Cann*)

In 1980 Gwent Theatre in Education Company re-enacted life at Tredegar House in the mid-nineteenth century. Gary Meredith played the part of the butler while Simon Scott and Liz Pearce acted as Charles and Rosemund Morgan. The pupils were from Croesyceiliog. (*Western Mail and Echo*)

End of an Era

This mosaic work by sculptor Sebastian Boysen was laid in Commercial
Street in 1995 to mark the fiftieth anniversary of the end of the Second
World War. (*Western Mail and Echo*)

A landmark sculpture beside the River Usk. (*Western Mail and Echo*)

The Baden-Powell Band at a civic service, mid-1990s. (*Western Mail and Echo*)

Youngsters demanding a Welsh language school for Newport in the early 1990s. (*Western Mail and Echo*)

When John Donovan retired as head of St Patrick's Primary School in 1995, it brought to an end four decades of service as a union representative for his profession. He was a former President of the Cardiff branch of the National Association of Schoolmasters and Women Teachers and also a member of the national executive. (*Western Mail and Echo*)

Welsh rugby international Arwel Thomas passes a Gwent TEC teachers' resources pack on manufacturing to former Pontypool star Geoff Davies, head teacher at Hartridge Comprehensive School. (*Western Mail and Echo*)

Youngsters enjoying themselves in 1998 at the Newport Super Karting centre on the Leeway Estate. (*Western Mail and Echo*)

When refugees from the Great Irish Famine arrived off Newport on a ship called the *Wanderer* in 1847, it was banned from docking. The refugees crawled across the mud of the River Usk to reach shore, and in some quarters Irish people in Newport are still known as the Mud Crawlers. But Irish tradition still thrives in the town, and these three youngsters are members of the O'Donnell School of Irish Dancing at the Portobello Club, seen here in 1996. (*Western Mail and Echo*)

Students at the University of Wales College in Newport made a twelve minute film in 1997, and managed to recruit Joseph Marcel, who plays the part of an English butler in the teenage American sitcom *The Fresh Prince of Bel Air*. (*Western Mail and Echo*)

Opera singer Horst Vetter, a former member of the Vienna Boys' Choir, with the Newport Boys' Choir at St David's Church, Park Place, 1998. (*Author's collection*)

The League of Friends presented the Royal Gwent Hospital with a heartbeat monitoring machine which cost more than £8,000, mid-1990s. (*Western Mail and Echo*)

Above, a Newport cattle auction watched by a knowledgeable crowd; and below, a monument that serves as a reminder of the town's long market tradition. (*Western Mail and Echo*)

Traders in Newport were unhappy about plans to pedestrianise the town centre. (*Western Mail and Echo*)

Pupils of Crindau and Clytha primary schools were chosen by the council to place images of the 1990s in a time capsule to be opened in 2045. (*Western Mail and Echo*)

Welsh Secretary David Hunt, standing to the right of the Mayor, Councillor Harry Jones, visited the town in July 1990 to see the plans of a proposed Usk Barrage, which were later rejected by his government. (*Western Mail and Echo*)

Celtic Manor Golf Club, a first-rate leisure facility. (*Western Mail and Echo*)

David Andrews, chairman of Castle Leisure, is cheered by builders as he lays the last brick at the Castle Bingo Hall, 1996. (*Western Mail and Echo*)

Toddlers at the Cylch Meithrin-y-Berllan playgroup, which meets at the St Julian Community Centre, start learning Welsh from the age of two, 1995. (*Western Mail and Echo*)

Newport High Street from Stow Hill in the 1990s. (*Author's collection*)

Fish and chips were on the menu when staff of Newport Library and Museum celebrated its 100th anniversary in 1988. (*Western Mail and Echo*)

Stilt-walker Mick Taylor entertaining the crowds in the shopping centre in 1994. (*Western Mail and Echo*)

An aerial view showing the Celtic Manor Hotel and golf course. (*Celtic Hotel Archives*)

Golfers Ian Woosnam and Mark James with Celtic Hotel and Golf Course owner Terry Matthews. (*Celtic Hotel Archives*)

Terry Matthews drinks a toast to the success of the new hotel at its official opening. (*Celtic Hotel Archives*)

St Woolos Primary School's history almost spanned the twentieth century. Head teacher Keith Beardmore is seen with some of his pupils when the school celebrated its 90th anniversary in 1994. (*Western Mail and Echo*)

The Leader of Newport Council, Sir Harry Jones, who was knighted for his services to local government. (*Western Mail and Echo*)

On 7 December 1999 the Rt Revd Rowan Douglas Williams, Bishop of Monmouth, was elected as the eleventh Archbishop of Wales and a few weeks later was enthroned at St Woolos Cathedral. Previous posts he held included that of tutor at the Theological College, Westcott House, in Cambridge, Lecturer in Divinity at Cambridge University and Lady Margaret Professor of Divinity at Christ Church College, Oxford. He was elected Bishop of Monmouth in 1991. (*David Williams*)

Acknowledgements

The author would like to thank the following for their contributions, help and support.

The *Western Mail and Echo* and the generations of photographers who worked for the newspapers; The Imperial War Museum; Gwent Record Office, Cwmbran; Newport County Borough Council and Newport Central Library; the Governing Body of the Church in Wales; Ivor Novello Foundation; Victoria Cross Association; Ted Milburn; Anthony Smith, author of *Survived*; Arthur K. Blood; Desmond C. Denny; Public Relations service; Leslie Hansen; Richard Cann; Celtic Hotel; the Sisters of St Joseph of Annécy; Marion Qua.

The new *Newport Pilot* seen at Newport Docks, c. 1960. (*Western Mail and Echo*)